DOUBLE STOP BEGINNINGS FOR VIOLA

BOOK ONE

BY CASSIA HARVEY

CHP251

©2014 by C. Harvey Publications All Rights Reserved.
6403 N. 6th Street
Philadelphia, PA 19126
www.charveypublications.com

Suggestions to Improve Sound

1. Press the fingers of the left hand down firmly.
2. Make sure the fingers are in tune.
   Weaker fingers need special attention so that the sound is not flat.
3. Balance the bow evenly across the two strings in each double stop.
4. Play *mf* or *mp* so you can hear the notes clearly. Rather than playing louder to get both strings to sound, balance your bow evenly between the two strings.
5. Keep the bow moving across the strings; don't get stuck.

Part 1

Cassia Harvey

Waltz

Double Stop Tune

Part 2

Double Stop Beginnings for the Viola, Book One

Playing Two Double Stops in a Row

Double Stop Study

Part 3

Crossing Strings

Double Stop Fiddle Tune

Double Stop Beginnings for the Viola, Book One

Fiddle Tune: Devil's Dream

©2014 C. Harvey Publications All Rights Reserved.

Part 4

Folk Tune: The Yellow Haired Laddie

Folk Tune: Polly, Put the Kettle On

Switching Double Stops

Clarke's Prince of Denmark March

Fiddle Tune: Arkansas Traveler

Part 6

Skipping Notes

Fiddle Tune: Turkey in the Straw

Fiddle Tune: Soldier's Joy

Double Stop Beginnings for the Viola, Book One

Part 7

Building a Scale in Double Stops

English Folk Tune

Fiddle Tune: Polly Wolly Doodle

Variation on an Etude by Spohr

Double Stop Study

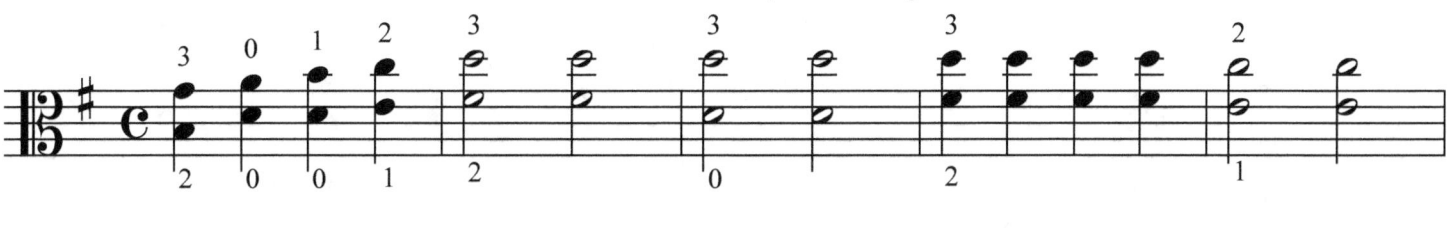
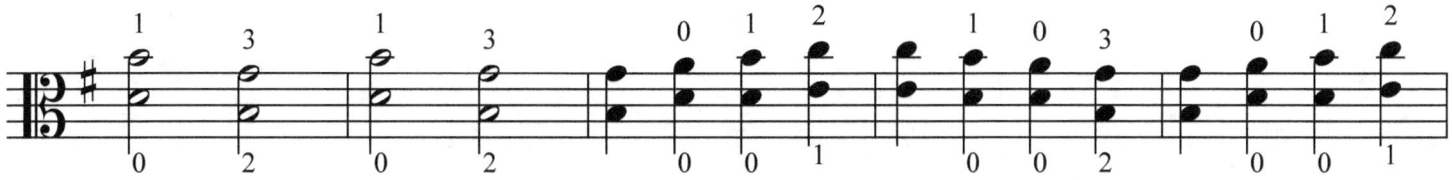

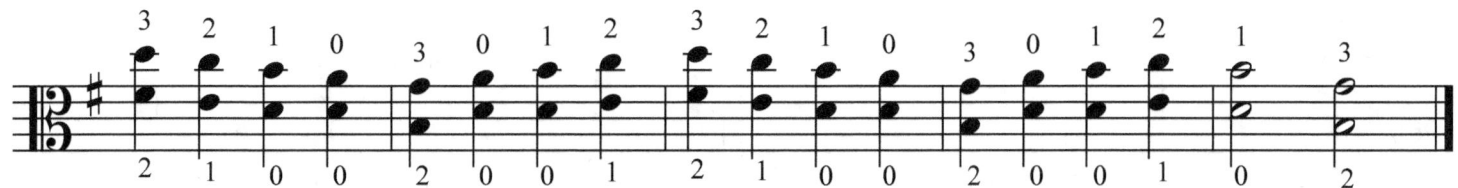

Fiddle Tune: John Ryan's Polka

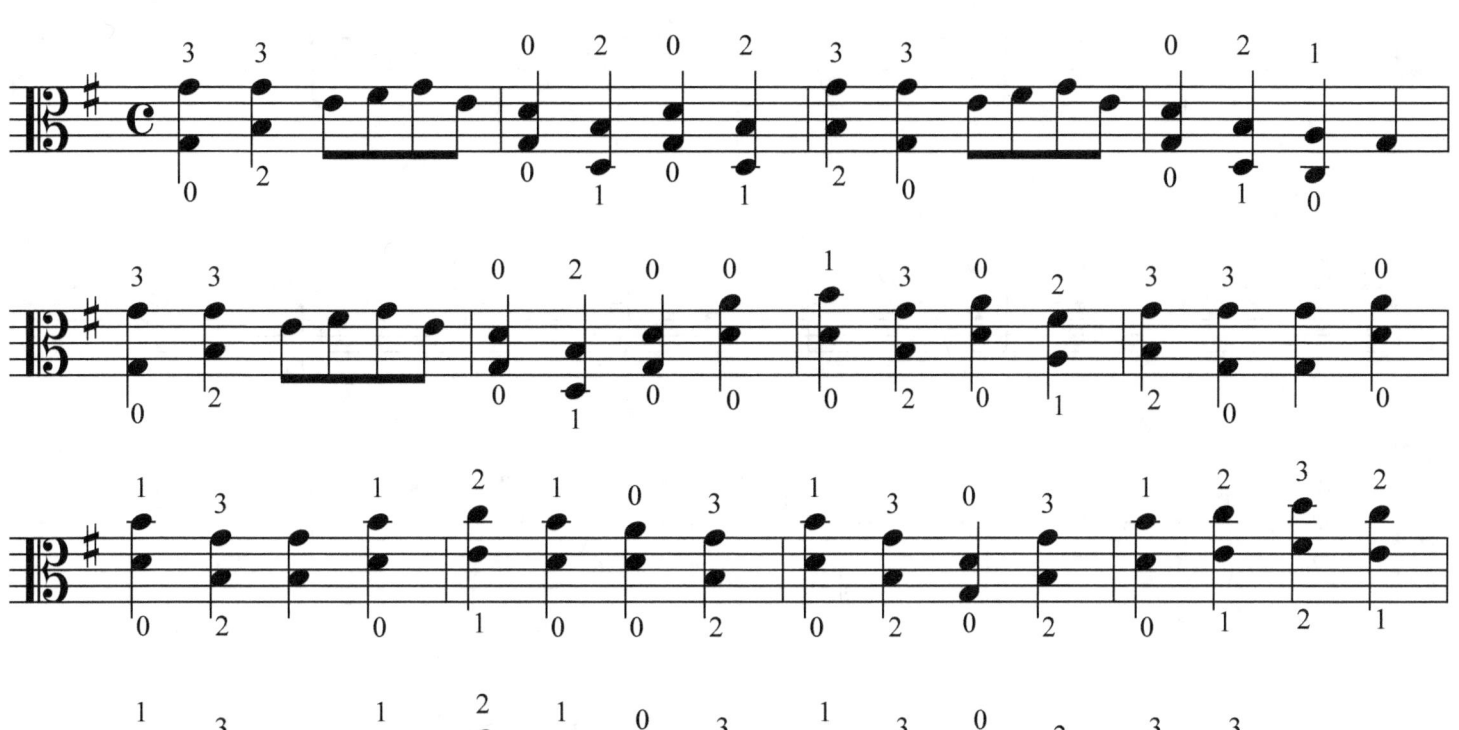

Bast's Contredanse

Part 9

Crossing Strings to 4th Finger

Fiddle Tune: Turkey in the Straw

Fiddle Tune: Mount Hills

Part 10

Skipping Notes

Irish Fiddle Tune: The Galway Piper

Barbarini's Tambourine

Double Stop Beginnings for the Viola, Book One

©2014 C. Harvey Publications All Rights Reserved.

Fiddle Tune: Colonel Gordon's Minuet

available from www.charveypublications.com: CHP268

Flying Fiddle Duets for Two Violas, Book One

John Ryan's Polka

Trad., arr. Myanna Harvey

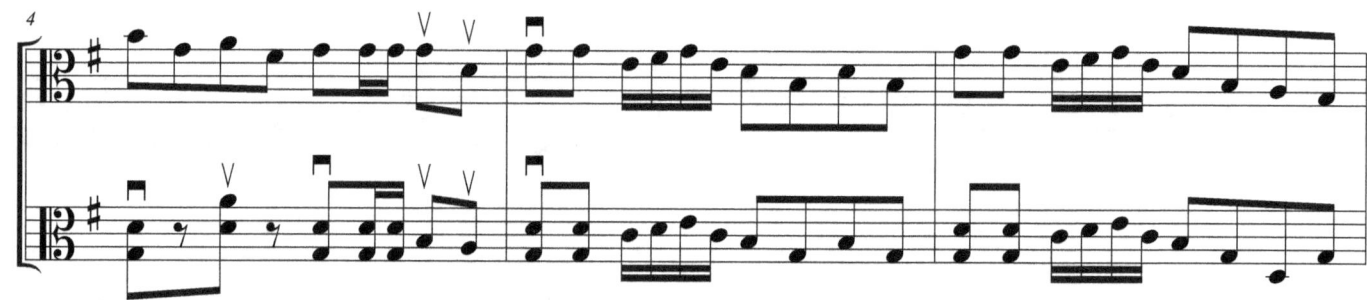

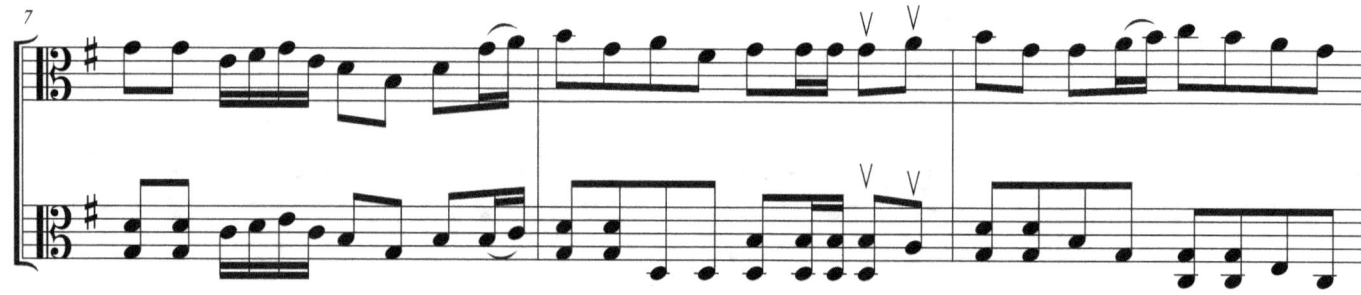

©2015 C. Harvey Publications. All Rights Reserved.

www.ingramcontent.com/pod-product-compliance
Lightning Source LLC
Chambersburg PA
CBHW051428070526
44584CB00023B/3635